THE TYNE OARSMEN

HARRY CLASPER • ROBERT CHAMBERS • JAMES RENFORTH

by

PETER DILLON

Published by:
Keepdate (Publishing) Ltd
21 Portland Terrace
Jesmond
Newcastle upon Tyne
NE2 1QQ

First edition 1993

ISBN 0-9520494-3-0

Designed & typeset by Keepdate Ltd
Newcastle upon Tyne

Printed by The Alden Press, Oxford

$$\boxed{\textit{Dedicated to the Tyne}}$$

CONTENTS

ACKNOWLEDGEMENTS

David Clasper HARRY CLASPER, HERO OF THE NORTH.
Published by Gateshead Books (Portcullis Press).

Eric Halladay ROWING IN ENGLAND:
A SOCIAL HISTORY. THE AMATEUR DEBATE.
Published by Manchester University Press.

Keith Gregson NORTH EAST LABOUR HISTORY.

Photographs courtesy of
David Clasper's collection.

INTRODUCTION

On a cold, bright, autumn day in 1988, 'Wor' Jackie Milburn, the famous Newcastle United No 9, who had inspired the team to three F.A. Cup victories in the 1950s, was buried. As the cortege wound its way towards the city's St Mary's Cathedral crowds lined the route, city centre traffic came to a standstill and men reminded of their youth shed tears. Milburn had been laid to rest amongst the people who had revered his name and kissed the grass he played on. He was the latest in a long line of North Eastern sportsmen, who had been given a hero's burial.

Although much smaller in scale, Milburn's final journey was a scene that echoed the extravagant funerals of the Tyne oarsmen, Harry Clasper, Robert Chambers and James Renforth over a hundred years before. At a time when rowing had been even more popular than football is today, the oarsmen became the first Geordie folk heroes. Immortalised in verse and song, arguably they are amongst the greatest sportsmen this country has ever produced, but it's likely that most people today have never heard of them. Yet, if the attendance at Harry Clasper's funeral in 1870 was any measure of his popularity, then he will never be beaten. That was how he liked it on the water, too. 'Clasper never knew when he was licked', reported one commentator.

An estimated 100,000 to 130,000 people lined the route from the Tunnel Inn, near the mouth of the River Ouseburn, where he had died, to his burial place at St Mary's Church in Whickham. The original plan had been to take the coffin overland, but the cortege stuck fast amongst the crowds on the Sandhill, and even though extra constables were brought in to move the thousands of enthusiastic mourners, there was no way through. Fittingly, the coffin was placed aboard a barge beneath the High

Level Bridge, and as a hymn sung by choristers at the Mansion House floated across the water, Clasper was rowed up the Tyne.

The crowds hanging off the bridges, packing the haughs (riverbanks) and following in a flotilla of boats, were evidence enough of a demi God worshipped on his way to Valhalla. Chambers' funeral two years earlier had also drawn massive crowds along the route from Pottery Bank in St Anthony's to Walker Cemetery. Flags on the boats of the Tyne General Ferry Company flew at half mast and the bell of St Nicholas' Church boomed out at a sonorous death march pace. Renforth's death in 1871 was all the harder to bear for being so sudden and so far away in Canada. His dying words were reputed to be, 'What will they say in England ?'

In 'The Deeth of Renforth' Rowland Harrison supplied the answer:

'Ye cruel Atlantic cable,
What's myed ye bring such fearful news?
When Tyneside's hardly yeble
Such sudden grief to bide.
Hoo me heart it beats – iv'rybody greets,
As the whisper runs throo dowley streets
"We've lost poor Jimmy Renforth,
The champein o' Tyneside!"

These then were the famous Tyne oarsmen, and when they died an era went with them. Professional rowing on the river was never the same again. Though the songs still exist describing their exploits on the water, the accounts of their funerals, and the elaborate statues marking their graves, Clasper, Chambers and Renforth are now the forgotten heroes of Tyneside. They are the men whose brilliance crystallised the region's obsession with sport, and it's from the oarsmen that Tynesiders inherit their love of sporting heroes. The crowd's applause for skill, determination and

APRIL 1882. Race for Sculling Championship, Newcastle.

commitment to the cause, still very much in evidence from the terraces at St James' Park, is a legacy from the rowing days. No longer do the fans stand on the banks of the 'coaly Tyne' watching skiffs racing by, but thrill instead to the sight of strikers lashing the ball into the back of the net. The sport may be different, but the passion is the same.

Despite the enormous changes in people's circumstances, expectations and aspirations since the mid nineteenth century, the spirit of the oarsmen has been carried forward. Brendan Foster and Steve Cram on the track running for the line, and at Gallowgate, Peter Beardsley and Chris Waddle dancing through opposing defences during Newcastle United's triumphant promotion season in 1984. And in May, 1993, Lee Clark, the North East's Footballer of the Year, crowning a brilliant campaign at St James' Park by driving the side to the First Division Championship. The week of rejoicing that followed this victory harked back to

the carnival atmosphere in the town when the rowers were successful. Lastly, of course, the very special skill of Paul Gascoigne, who has a particular link with the Tyne oarsmen. Clasper and Gascoigne were both born in Dunston.

GROWTH AND DEVELOPMENT

As might be expected money was a major factor in the growth and development of professional rowing on the River Tyne. Prize money for the winners, the crowds betting on the outcome of the races and the backers or sponsors putting up the stake money for the crews. All in all it could be an expensive business.

At the start of the nineteenth century races would have come about in an ad hoc way, the result of a bet between friends or even enemies, and boatmen literally messing about on the river. But by the

1830s the beginning of professional rowing's golden age, river racing had become much more organised and lucrative for the sponsors and successful oarsmen. Clasper's purse throughout his career was an estimated £2,600.

The enterprise provided a perfect division of responsibility between capital and labour. The sponsors were local businessmen and influential figures, amongst them the most distinguished being Joseph Cowen, the radical M.P. and owner of the Newcastle Courant, and William Hutt, the M.P. for Gateshead. Masonic symbols decorate Chambers' monument in Walker Cemetery, so it's a sure bet the local lodges were behind the famous sculler. For their part, the oarsmen were hewn from the industrial communities developing on both banks of the Tyne. Clasper came from a mining family, Chambers was an ironworker and Renforth worked as a ferryman and foundry worker. Public houses played an important role in the history of river racing. Matches between rival crews were often hatched in pubs, and the stake money for the races deposited with the publicans or the matchmaker. Rowing and drink were further entwined by boathouses built onto the end of pubs, and sometimes it was hard to tell if there was any difference between the two establishments. Pubs were also the location for fierce argument and banter on the merits of this crew against that one, and the publicans themselves were keen spotters of new talent.

Towards the end of his career some of Clasper's friends and backers clubbed together to raise the money to buy him what was to become The Clasper Hotel, a public house on Armstrong Road in Newcastle. In all Clasper ran eight pubs, including The Skiff at Derwenthaugh, and the Barley Mow at Sandgate, both of which still exist, but are considerably changed since Clasper's tenancy. Bob Chambers had The King's Head on

Pottery Bank in Walker. Since then it's become a tradition for professional sportsmen to retire from their game and run pubs. Today 'Clasper's Bar' at the Copthorne Hotel on Newcastle Quayside helps keep the tradition alive.

Drink has continued to play an important part behind the scenes in sport. Newcastle Breweries influenced the creation of Newcastle United in 1892, and to this day operate sponsorship schemes, which have helped them secure the services of the likes of Kevin Keegan as a player and latterly as a manager. They have also provided Durham County Cricket Club with its most illustrious member to date, Ian Botham. Not to be outdone, Vaux Breweries on the banks of the River Wear have regularly backed Sunderland A.F.C.

The rowers' prime on the river coincided with the emergence of Newcastle as a manufacturing and industrial base. Armstrong established his factory at Elswick in the 1840s and shipbuilding yards, mines and engineering works, ingredients of the Victorian boom, occupied sites on the banks of the Tyne parallel with the boat race course, which ran from the High Level Bridge to Scotswood Suspension Bridge or Lemington Point. So, geographically, professional rowing and industry were further locked together.

The rowers' success became a symbol of Newcastle's burgeoning confidence at the centre of the industrial revolution, and for thousands of ordinary people a source of immense pride. These workers grinding out an existence in the sweat shops and foundries so identified with the oarsmen, in some cases their own work mates, that regatta day was the one moment in their lives when they could stand tall and claim the victory belonged to them. Verses from 'The One Mile Race – July 1863' gives an indication of the sport's popularity amongst both male and female:

BOAT RACE. Scotswood Bridge, Newcastle.

Wor Jack an Tom, alang wi' me,
Join'd i' the hurry skurry
That sped alang Newcassel Kee,
When foaks with frantic flurry
Rush'd here an' there te get a place
That they might see the greet boat race;
Alang the Close they madly push'd,
Byeth foaks an' people sair wes crush'd,
An' poor sowl's feet that sported CORN,
Wes nice an' clean tho ruffly shorn,
When they te see the race, lads.

On the river – a'sorts o' craft,
Frae whurry te the steamer,
Wes crooded weel byeth fore and aft,–
Mind, mark ye, aw's ne dreamer,
The banks and bridges – sic a seet,
For lads wes scramblin' left and reet,
An' lasses wi' thor bonny goons,
An' greet big hats wi' little croons,
Join'd i' mony a queer like crew,

That they might get a better view,
An' see the greet boat race, lads.

It was as though through their success Clasper, Chambers and Renforth could speak for a whole northern underclass, and if they beat a London crew, the triumph was so much the sweeter. The first ones to achieve that joy in a major race were Harry Clasper's crew, but there was a great deal of blood, sweat and tears before that day.

It should be said that not everyone in the North East was sports mad and captivated by the oarsmen. One landlady remarked of rowing, "Two men wi' nae claes on, pulling for bare life on lang planks o' wood".

Wor Peg, a character devised by the monologist, Joe Wilson, offered the following advice. "It wad be a vast better if boat rowers wes to pull wi' thor heeds turn'd the tuther way, so they cud see where thor gannin te".

However, these views were in the minority.

"HAUD AWAY, HARRY"

'A man so various that he seem'd to be not one, but all mankind's epitome'.

The poet Dryden's words could well have described Harry Clasper at the peak of his powers. This moment could be pinpointed as the 26th June, 1845 when his skills as a brilliant oarsman, leader of men, and boat designer and builder, came together in a race to produce one of the best performances in the history of professional rowing. At the Thames Regatta, Harry and his four oar crew of brothers were pitched against the might of the London Watermen for the rowing championship of the World. For the record, the Geordies were given no hope – but Clasper's story begins long before that summer's day.

The foundations for Harry Clasper's success were laid early on in his life. His childhood was spent amongst the boats and small crafts on the busy Tyne and in his teens he served an apprenticeship as a carpenter in a boatyard. But the key to Clasper's great abilities was his willingness to learn from his experiences.

He was born in 1812, in Dunston, then a small village on the south side of the river about a mile upstream from the centre of Newcastle. Later when the family moved to Jarrow, near the mouth of the Tyne, the fifteen year old Clasper began his working life at Jarrow Pit. But his career in mining only lasted a fortnight. A violent explosion underground rapidly persuaded the young Clasper to seek more 'genial employment'. This he found

HARRY CLASPER.
From a lithograph published by Newbold, Strand.

when he joined Brown's boatyard – later to become the famous Palmers ship building yard. It was a logical step for Clasper, who as a youngster had built his own boat. A sign of things to come. Brown singled him out as an above average pupil, who was always willing to listen and learn. From Brown the enthusiastic apprentice learned the rudiments of boat design and construction.

After the great pit strike of 1831 the Clasper family was on the move again – returning to Dunston. It was here, back at his birthplace that Harry Clasper's rowing career began. Rowing at stroke, the captain's traditional position in the boat, Clasper led his crew of brothers, William and Robert (cox) and Jack Thompson and Hobbie (Robert) Dinning. Racing in a boat called the *Swalwell* – named after a village near Dunston – they were referred to as the Derwenthaugh crew. This was because they rowed on the Derwent, which flows into the Tyne, and Clasper was working as a wherryman (bargee) and coke burner at the Garesfield Coke Company at Derwenthaugh (not far from the present day site of Metro Radio). The victory that brought his crew to public notice was against the much more favoured *Country Lass* from Swalwell. Although the prize money of approximately £10.00 was relatively small, the kudos was much greater, and for Clasper much sweeter as his crew had started the race as underdogs. Coming from behind and winning would be repeated later, and a theme Clasper would share with another great Tyne oarsman, Bob Chambers.

As the crew went from strength to strength and proved a match for any opposition in the North East, Clasper's domestic life provided vital support for his professional ambitions. In 1836 he married his cousin, Susannah Hawks, who was connected to the Hawks family, owners of the foundry on the site (approximately) of what is now Gateshead stadium. Given Clasper's desire to be the best on the river, it is certainly true that a marriage which brought him into contact with money would help enormously. Cash was always needed for (amongst other things) boat maintenance and repair, stake money for races and as crews became more successful and broadened their horizons, travel. Whilst it is not known to what extent Susannah's relations directly helped Clasper on the river, at one stage an uncle provided 'pecuniary aid' and for a short spell he worked at the Hawks, Crawshay & Sons Ironworks.

The Derwenthaugh crew progressed to rowing a boat called the *St Agnes* built by the esteemed boat builder, John Dobson of Hillgate, Gateshead. (Not to be confused with the architect, John Dobson of the same period, who had just re-designed the centre of Newcastle.) The *St Agnes*, the Tyne Watermen – keepers of the faith in all things nautical – agreed was the fastest boat in the

HENRY CLASPER,

(INVENTOR OF THE PRESENT OUTRIGGER,

Boat Builder,

"ROWER'S ARMS," LOW ELSWICK,

NEWCASTLE-ON-TYNE.

N.B—Boats of every description Built to order.

BOATS LET OUT BY THE DAY OR HOUR.

SCULLERS' BOATS BUILT ON THE SHORTEST NOTICE.

north. Many observers ascribed the crew's success to the quality of their boat, which in effect rather diminished the contribution of the rowers. A view which in the light of what was to happen gave rise to much debate. Not to be outdone though in the designing and boat construction stakes, Clasper, using the skills he had learned at Brown's, produced a craft called *The Hawk* and a year later, *The Young Hawk*, both sculls, in which he pursued a solo career and won the Durham Regatta cup. These craft were significant because they were the first Clasper boats built to compete professionally and they were successful.

Meanwhile, the Derwenthaugh crew in the *St Agnes* were virtually unbeatable. It was time to chance their arm further afield. The crowds were fully behind Clasper's men and had come to believe they were invincible. Possibly even Clasper wondered this when he threw down the gauntlet to race any crew, from anywhere, at any time.

To Clasper's delight, the formidable national champions, the London Watermen, accepted the challenge. This was proof he was within an ace of joining the big league – just win this race and the horizon was endless. His supporters were delighted, here was the chance to show those southerners a thing or two. If anything the north/south divide was probably even more marked than it is today. The foe were coming to the Tyne for a ducking; the north would soon show the south who was King of the River. Amidst all the anticipation and fervour there was of course the prospect of a quite different result, but no one on the Tyne would even bring themselves to consider such a possibility.

The race was fixed for July 16th, 1842, from Newcastle Bridge to Lemington and the stakes arranged at £150-a-side. The London crew led by their non rowing captain, Lord Kilmorey, numbered Newall, Coombes and the

Doubledees J. and R. These were rowers drawn from the ranks of the Thames Lightermen (watermen), working folk much like their northern counterparts. They travelled north, probably aware of the frosty reception that was in store, but nevertheless determined to snuff out the challenge from the Geordie upstarts.

Much to the horror of the massed crowds, snuff out the local heroes is precisely what the Londoners did. It probably was not the easiest race they ever had, but the Derwenthaugh crew never really posed them any serious threat. The Watermen coasted home in 29 minutes proving to one and all that they were worthy champions.

For Harry Clasper it was the hardest lesson of his life, and the full force of his crew's defeat fell on him. He was the one who had made the challenge, brought the Watermen north to fight it out on his river, the setting of so many of his victories, and now he was the one who had been beaten. And, to make matters worse, it had happened in front of his people, his crowd, his faithful supporters. There were plenty there that day who had invested so much emotionally in Harry Clasper that they must have felt he had let them down. If their own dreams and aspirations could never come true, then their hopes for Harry surely would. Now it must have seemed to them even that was unlikely. As well as his own desperate disappointment Clasper will have been all too well aware of the crowd's dismay. Then of course there were the thousands who had placed bets on the local crew and, as a result, were feeling the poorer and very sore.

But Clasper refused to surrender. He claimed his crew were just as good oarsmen as the Londoners, and that they had been beaten by a superior boat. "We weren't beaten by the rowing," he said, "we were beaten by the boat."

MAY 1867. Great Boat Race, Newcastle. Finish of race, Lemington Point.

The claim did have substance – if anyone could be bothered to listen. Clasper did what he always did best, going back to basics and learning. While everyone else was in shock at the result, Clasper was studying the Londoners' boat. It was lighter than the *St Agnes*, swam higher in the water, and the crew used curved oars. Clasper was more and more convinced his initial reaction was right, and whatever anyone else thought, said or did, he was determined to build a new boat and defeat the cockneys. The key was to make it as light as possible so his crew could row it through the water as quickly as possible.

Most people were not interested. There was nothing more embarrassing than a deposed idol still shouting the odds. As far as the public were concerned the Derwenthaugh crew had reached their top mark. In the north they had proved they were the best in the water, but in the larger pool they had been found wanting. In other words, the Claspers could not compete with the best – the champions.

Whenever Clasper did find anyone prepared to listen to his ideas, he was ridiculed. Men who worked on the river, or in the heavy industries were used to sturdy, hardy boats. These craft were the tried and tested tools of their trade, and a flimsy boat was beneath their consideration. For one thing it would never float, and for another it would sink, or get blown over in the wind. And, worst of all perhaps, it just did not look manly enough.

In spite of what must have felt like universal disregard, Clasper locked himself inside a boathouse called Paradise, on the Tyne, and hammered out his new design. This was his own cottage industry amidst the factories and foundries developing around him. He was adamant; he was not going to make a copy of the London boat, but

JULY 1866. International Boat Race on the Tyne at Newcastle.

rather use theirs as his stepping off point. The lightness was only the start. By removing the keel from the outside to the inside to increase speed the boat looked keel-less. Next, he improved and developed the mechanism which held the oars in place, the outrigger. This had been invented earlier, but Clasper extended the rig beyond the body of the boat to give the oar more pull and thus give the boat even more speed. The completed boat, christened *The Five Brothers* and shaped like half a gun barrel, was a revelation. Nothing quite like it had ever been seen before. Clasper's design became the prototype for all modern racing boats, but that was later. In the meantime he had the cockneys to beat.

The new boat was one thing, the readiness of the crew for the fray was another. To master rowing *The Five Brothers* they needed to put in hours of practice and be in mint condition. Clasper, a keen coach put them through his own devised training schedules adapted to suit each individual. It is doubtful that the following are his exact words, but his philosophy amounted to as much. "It's folly to attempt to train a man by any set of rules. Some men who are not in good condition require good feeding and moderate work to bring them up to the mark. The work must be regulated according to the constitution and habits of the man, and the food to a certain extent must be adapted in a similar manner."

However, Clasper insisted on his rowers keeping regular hours, preferring them to be up by seven in the morning and in bed again by ten at night. Three good meals a day was considered 'temperate and a proper allowance' though the third meal was only to consist of tea and toast lightly buttered with an egg on top. In extreme cases a crew member's weight could be adjusted quickly before a race. This was achieved by the man wearing double the clothing during walking and hard training exercises. At night he would sleep beneath extra layers of bedding and be rubbed down until dry in the morning. In other words, a regime of exercising and sweating off the flab. It was a routine to be handled with great care and only recommended if there was no other way. Training sessions would involve using weights, walking, running and rowing on the river. Doubtless a routine that is familiar to today's oarsmen.

The Five Brothers proved a success on the water, but still Clasper was not satisfied. There was no purpose going in against the Watermen until everything was perfect. Refinements were made and tried out, some were used, others dropped. Finally, seeking the ultimate in boat design and construction Clasper decided to improve on *The Five Brothers* and emerged with the *Lord Ravensworth*. This was built on the same principles as the previous craft, but many considered the new boat the finest Harry Clasper had ever made. The

crowds that had discarded and disowned him now came back to the fold. But he still had everything to prove, and the cockneys hearing and seeing the technical advances made on the Tyne had not been idle. They had been busy adapting and slimming down their boats to meet the challenge.

All was set for the race between north and south to decide the rowing championship of the World. It was June 26th, 1845, almost three years since Clasper had been humiliated on the Tyne. It had been a hard struggle to get back in contention, but now he was finally ready to do battle on the Thames. Clasper's crew on that momentous day was Harry at stroke, his brothers, William, Robert and Richard, and replacing Edward Clasper, who had sadly died that April, Ned Hawks, Harry's uncle and affectionately known as the old 'un. In the finals, the *Lord Ravensworth* was matched against two crews, one led by Pocock and known as the London crew, and the other captained by

Robert Coombes, who had done so much to unseat Clasper on the Tyne.

For the Geordies it was now or never. At the start of the regatta their boat had been greeted by disbelief and laughter, but as they progressed through the heats, grudging admiration filtered through the London crowd. Still no one gave them a chance. But in their boat Clasper's crew felt all they had to do was row at their best to take the championship back to the Tyne.

There was controversy at the starting line. Mr Bishop, the umpire, declared that the crews had gone before he had given the signal, and spent much of the race trying to get it abandoned. This eagerness to start only underlined the crews' commitment and no one was going to stop Clasper's men until they had passed the finishing post, preferably first. The crews, well matched, were oar to oar in the opening stages. Then

Coombes, probably mindful of the psychological advantage he enjoyed over Clasper, tried to spurt into the lead. Clasper watched cautiously and waited, he was not going to be hurried. He and his crew knew exactly what they were doing – after all, hadn't they rowed this race in their heads many times before? It did not matter what Coombes or Pocock did, it was up to the northerners to row their own race.

Then at Hammersmith Bridge, no doubt sensing the whole of Tyneside holding its breath and willing them on, the Claspers and the old 'un began drawing ahead. First a length, and then another; Coombes seeing the race slipping away from him fought back, but this was not to be his day and he only managed to knock half a length off the Geordies' lead. The crew of the *Lord Ravensworth* rowed on supremely confident in themselves and their boat. Coombes and Pocock were forgotten, the defeat on the Tyne obliterated.

Only a clear stretch of water lay ahead of them, and vindication of all that Harry Clasper stood for. His leadership qualities, his brilliance with the oar, his designing and construction skills, and last but not least his training methods were all in evidence that day on the Thames. Clasper stroked his crew past the winning post to become Champions of the World. He and his crew had come from so far behind that even some of their supporters had written them off, but in the ecstasy of victory all that was forgotten. The Claspers were now Kings of the River – any river. Lord Kilmorey, the Londoners' backer rowed alongside the Claspers dispensing wine, which they mistook for port. Who cared?

One commentator was later moved to write: 'The greatest name in aquatic circles is that of Harry Clasper...what Frederick the Great was in matters military, Harry is in boat racing. He was never discouraged by a defeat, but always learned

STATUE OF HARRY CLASPER. Made by Richard Haddrick, June 18, 1859.

from it something which carried him on to future victories'.

The same scribe, now in rhapsody, quoted from 'Othello':

> 'Another of his fashion, they have not
> To lead their business'.

On the crew's return to Newcastle, the town went wild – just as they would years later when the football team came back from Wembley with the F.A. Cup. Only the man himself, Harry Clasper, was missing from the glorious homecoming. He had stayed in London to sell the *Lord Ravensworth* to Lord Kilmorey for £81.00 and pick up commissions to build other boats.

Clasper and his victorious crew were now held in such high esteem by their supporters, that they had become as popular as musicians in the latter half of the twentieth century. It could be argued that the Victorian rowers were the nineteenth century version of pop stars. Certainly songs were written about them, none more devoted than J.P. Robson's:

> 'Ov a' your grand rowers in skiff or in skull,
> There's nyen wi' wor Harry has chance for to pull
> Man he sits like a duke an' he fetchrs se free,
> Oh! Harry's the lad, Harry Clasper for me!
>
> HAUD AWAY, HARRY! CANNY LAD, HARRY!
> HARRY'S THE KING OF THE TYEMS AN'
> THE TYNE.
>
> Harry smothers them a' for he beels his awn boat;
> But nyen like hissel, man, can set her afloat
> He cuts through the Tyne like a fish i' the sea
> An the lasses a' shoot, as he shuts by the key,
> HAUD AWAY, HARRY! MAW DARLIN',
> HARRY!'

In the years following the championship win, Clasper and his crew did not sit on their laurels. How could they; there was a reputation to live up to – they were the rowers every crew wanted to beat. Despite the pressure to stay on top, Clasper did find time to bring in new oarsmen. In a way he was probably looking for someone to inherit his crown. The sculler, Bob Chambers, caught his eye and prospered from Clasper's coaching. The two became great friends, and although Chambers was sadly to die before Clasper, he did take on his mentor's crown.

Towards the end of his career, Harry Clasper was fixed forever in Tyneside mythology by a song that had nothing to do with river racing. On June 5th, 1862, Clasper was treated to a testimonial evening at Balmbra's Music Hall in Newcastle's Cloth Market. This was a way for Clasper's friends, supporters and backers to say a public thank you to the great oarsman. By all accounts the jugglers and musicians helped to turn it into a riotous evening. In retrospect, the high spot was the local songwriter and singer, Geordie Ridley, who presented several new songs, one of which was 'The Blaydon Races'. This later became Newcastle United's anthem, and can still be heard at St James' Park.

Premiered at Clasper's testimonial the song provides yet another link between the old Tyneside rowers and the new sporting heroes of today.

'HONEST BOB'

They say scullers (single oarsmen) are mad, so perhaps it follows that the maddest are the best. That would have made 'Honest Bob' Chambers, the Champion of the World certifiable, and his performance against White of Bermondsey in April 1859, is proof positive of obsessive behaviour.

Though, in his defence, it must be said that commentators have regarded this race as the greatest individual exhibition of rowing in the history of the sport.

At the best of times rowing is a hard business requiring strength, stamina and enormous will. Oarsmen need all the help they can get, and this comes mostly from themselves. For example, as in any group enterprise, a successful four oar crew create a unit greater than the individual parts, binding together as one against the opposition. As part of a team the members depend on each other and encourage one another. This is the internal support and drive mechanism that can push a crew to great heights.

But for a sculler things are different: he is on his own, he stands or falls by his own performance. If he makes a mistake, or fails at any moment there is no one else to help him put it right, rescue him,

make it better and encourage him. He trains alone on cold, dark, wet mornings and rows alone. Sculling is a test of character and exposes any shortcomings. There is no escape for the sculler, neither from the spectators watching his every move, nor – more importantly – from himself. So it takes a man with courage and honesty to be a sculler, and perhaps the greatest there has ever been was Bob Chambers.

He was born at St Anthony's, Walker, in Newcastle upon Tyne in 1831. He worked in an iron foundry before his skills on the river were fully recognised. At the age of twenty one he made his first public appearance and suffered a defeat. An inauspicious beginning, but scullers are nothing if not obstinate and it did not take long for Chambers to find winning ways and impress the Geordie crowds. 'Gan on, Bob,' was the cry that soon rent the air.

Chambers was an unassuming fellow, who

probably went so far as to under-rate his own performances. According to all reports he made rowing look easy, gliding his scull down the Tyne in the forty solo contests of his career, of which he won thirty four. Although obviously there is no film available to check these skills for ourselves, and precious little photography, there are the songs, stories and patter of the writers and music hall comedians, who sometimes describe a race in great detail. In today's terms, these accounts resemble live radio commentaries of football matches and thinking of the patter, even ball by ball reporting of cricket matches. The songs and drolleries of Joe Wilson, Ned Corvan and many others are a valuable resource, and not only for supplying the results of races, but for taking the emotional temperature of the crowd and giving an indication of the humour of the day. Here's a moment from 'The One Mile Race' about a match in 1863 between our man, Robert Chambers and Robert Cooper:

'HONEST BOB'.
From August 12, 1865,
Illustrated Sporting News.

'Thor i' thor boats, a keelman cries –
Aw'll back Bob for a ginney.
Which Bob? says aw, when he replies –
The Bob that wins maw hinney.

These verbatim reports also paint in – sometimes with the help of etchings and drawings from the London Illustrated News – the chaos on the river at the time of the races. Not for the Tynesiders the clear water organisation of a Henley or an Olympic Games contest. Increasingly the Tyne was a working river, and as more and more industry grew up on the banks the water would be packed with sailing boats, craft, wherries, barges and keels. Come a regatta or a race day, many of these would be commandeered by spectators attempting to follow the race afloat. It is probable that some of the helmsmen at the wheel were at best drunk, or incompetent, or even in the excitement of the moment just incapable. There was never any suggestion that they should follow in an orderly queue behind the rowers. That was just not possible. From their berths along the race course the craft would be cast off into mid stream. Given the pilot's hazy sense of direction and the industrial flotsam and jetsam jagging up in the water, the rowers had to have their wits about them.

For a description of the famous Tyne encounter between Chambers and the Londoner, Tom White, which a Newcastle paper described as 'one of the greatest triumphs that has ever been achieved' in the sporting world, we are indebted to the wit and reporting style of the Liverpool born, but Newcastle bred Ned Corvan and Joe Wilson. But particulars first; it was April 19th, 1859, and the race for £100-a-side was from the High Level Bridge, the three miles to Scotswood Suspension Bridge (Chambers' obituary puts the sum at £200-a-side). Like the great Clasper races, a Geordie was again matched against a Cockney, and once more the banks of the Tyne were packed with people hopeful of another northern victory.

According to Corvan, from the start there was nothing between the two oarsmen:

> *'Stroke for stroke contending they sweep on wi' the tide*
> *Fortune seems intending, the victor ti decide.'*

But then, just before the half mile mark off Skinnerburn, disaster struck for Chambers, and Corvan is in no doubt that White, weakening, commits what might be termed a professional foul:

> *'At last the cockney losing strength,*
> *the fowlin' game did steal*
> *He leaves his wettar ivery length,*
> *an runs Chambers iv a keel.'*

The net effect was that White crowded Chambers, who was rammed into a keel and spun round so that

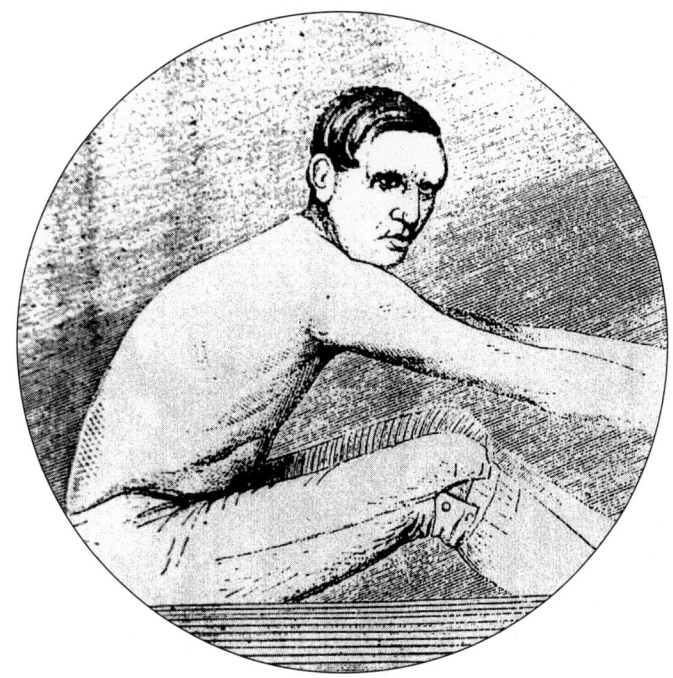

BOB CHAMBERS.
From a lithograph published by Newbold, Strand.

he was facing in the wrong direction. In 'Bob Chambers – A Dream And A Reality' Joe Wilson takes up the story;

'Then away the Cockney went above a hundred yards before brave Bob could better his condition.'

Surely the race was over, and as might have been expected there was consternation amongst the spectators to see their man in such dire straits.

'What a hullabaloo!…Every yen thowt the race was ower and began the wawk hyem before the finish o' the race'.

In today's parlance it's rather like the fans seeing Newcastle United football team 5-0 down at home with only twenty minutes to go. They stream away from St James' Park stadium as though propelled by a fire alarm – and why should they stay, there is no hope of the team pulling back from such a trouncing. To the crowds on the banks of the Tyne that day, Chambers had no chance. But, as Joe Wilson recounts, the only one who did not agree with the general consensus was the only one who could do something about it – 'Honest Bob' Chambers.

'His boat was like a dart, a fish, a bird, an' seun it flew alang as swift as ivor. Away they went the Cockney leadin' still a hundred yards, just like a winner. An' ivrybody thowt him sure te be the victor. Except Bob Chambers.'

What happened next defied description, and for years afterwards people who had witnessed it could scarcely believe it. At this level of racing, White's lead of a hundred yards ordinarily would have put the race beyond doubt. But scullers are not ordinary – they are mad – and Chambers, as he set about reducing White's lead, clearly the maddest.

Joe Wilson again:

'An' Bob, the honest, manly, game an' true, had
nivvor thowt (to lose) – for wi' fresh vigour in his
great lang stroke he follow'd bravely, an' then foaks
saw the lion-heart o' Bob, the Tyneside Champein.
What White mun thowt aw nivvor yit cud tell when
he saw Bob gainin'. Gainin' at ivory stroke.'

People who had left the racecourse with faces as
long as fiddles, and tearing up their betting slips,
now ran back to see one of the finest, if not indeed
the greatest recovery and fightback in sport. Inch
by inch, and then yard by yard, Chambers clawed
back White's lead. The base of Tyneside must have
shaken as the crowd took hold and roared
Chambers on to Scotswood. Now length by length,
'Honest Bob' seemed to be drinking up the water
between them and the impossible was happening.
For White the bridge and the finishing post could
not come quickly enough, but for Chambers – hold

it back for just a little longer. And then the rowers
were level, one more push for Bob – he had come
this far, surely he could not lose it now. As the line
approached Chambers edged into the lead and
White, by this time probably in shock for he had
been able to watch his opponent's transformation,
had nothing left with which to counter. Incredibly
Chambers crossed the finishing line the winner,
and Tyneside erupted. As if winning was not
enough, strait laced, 'Honest Bob' suggested that
as there had been a foul he was willing to row the
race again. The vanquished White had the grace
to decline.

Joe Wilson recalled the race as if in a dream, as well
he might, and ends with the line – 'This was me
dream, an', man, aw liked the dream that faithfully
portray'd what aw had seen i' fifty-nine'. Wilson
also records a gentle piece of Geordie patter
humour which might have occurred many times
over after this race:

*'Coming doon eftor awl wis ower, aw meets one
i' wor cheps (an Irishman) they called Patrick,
but I called him Mick for shortness. He wouldn't
wait for the finish altho' he'd backed Bob. So ah
hailed him.*
"Hie, Mick. Who's forst ?"
*"Shure," says he, "the Londin man was forst half
way before the race wis quarther over."*
"Had on, Mick. Did ye lay owt on Bob ?"
*"By my soul I did! An' I'd like to lay this lump ov a
stick on his dhirty coco-nut. The next time I
speckulate on floatin' property may I be sthruck wid a
button on my upper lip as big as a clock face."*
"But Chambers is forst," says I.
*"Arah," humped Mick. "Didn't I tell ye he'd win
afore iver he started."'*

Chambers went from strength to strength and won
the World Sculling Championship against Green of
Australia in 1863. He also enjoyed several epic
races against his fellow Geordie, Robert Cooper,
their different styles described thus:

*'Bob Cooper's strokes wes short, but quick,
Se bonny, clean an' strengthy,
Whilst Chambers pulls, his man te lick,
Wi strokes byeth strang an' lengthy.'*

In the end, though, Bob Chambers pushed himself
too hard – being a sculler, perhaps this was
inevitable. There was always one more race, or one
more great victory to chase. His backers wanted it,
the crowds certainly did, and 'Honest Bob' could
never say no. But he was not well and on the river
his deterioration was clear for all to see. He had T.B.
and was advised not to carry on racing. At the age of
37 on June 4th, 1868, he died, and provided Tyneside
with the first of three great oarsmens' funerals.

A verse from 'The Deeth o' Bob Chambers' sums
up the Geordies' loss and their famous sculler's
character:

OCTOBER 1859. Championship Sculling on the Thames.

'Fareweel te the canny Bob Chambers, –
A man for his honesty famed;
Strite-forward, an' kind, noble-hearted –
Wor champein such qualities claim'd.
Ay, an' what's mair, we knaw he possess'd them;
Oh, then, hoo can we help but repine
For the hero that gain'd wor affecshun,
Like this brave hardy son o' the Tyne.'

RENFORTH

James Renforth's career, though very successful, left his supporters on the Tyne wondering what might have been. He was the third in the triumvirate of great oarsman, and at twenty nine the youngest to die. But if ever there was a figure born to be a star it was Jimmy Renforth. He was powerfully built with long arms, a deep chest and an immense width across the shoulders – he was perfectly formed for rowing. This fine torso was topped off with a sense of style in the sartorial department, and Renforth often sported a white hat. He would have been a must for both the sports writers and the fashion pages of today's tabloids. Shy in public, but once in company he knew well he was the life and soul of the party. A useful mix of the vulnerable and confident – both characteristics which go well together in the make up of attractive public figures.

By the time Renforth came to prominence on the river in the late 1860s, professional rowing was gaining an unpleasant reputation. Fouling on the water, upsetting opponents and generally trying to put one over on the other crew within reason came to be an accepted part of the game. But, possibly due to the money involved and the pressures therein, rowers and their backers were now taking drastic steps to destroy the opposition. Boats were tampered with – holes drilled along the waterline – and races reputedly fixed. An ugly climate

RENFORTH on the Tyne.

increasingly surrounded what had passed for sport.

The other more positive development that had a great effect on Renforth's career was that rowing had become an international sporting event, and he joined a crew that took part in the Anglo-Canadian boat races of this period. Both the transatlantic dimension and the cheating element featured in Renforth's last dramatic race in August 1871.

He was born in a cottage near Rabbit Banks on the Gateshead side of the river, and within a stone's throw of the Tyne. Like Chambers before him he worked in the local foundries and factories, but then his life took an exotic turn. He found himself far from industrial Tyneside and in the West Indies. Obviously the idea of foreign travel appealed early on in young Renforth's life. Except, it was not quite as simple as that. He had enlisted in the army and, as part of his duty, was serving in the Caribbean.

No doubt it would have suited Renforth's work mates slaving away in the foundries to be anywhere but Gateshead and the prospect of the West Indies must have felt like another planet. Perhaps it was the endless sunshine and sandy beaches that palled for Renforth, and he pined for the rainy streets of Tyneside, or perhaps it was the uniformed rigours of army life that were not to his taste. In any event his father bought him out of the army and he returned to Gateshead.

Even before Renforth found fame as a rower he was no stranger to success on the water. He had won a gold medal for swimming at the Northumberland Baths and after leaving the army in 1866 he was back on the water. He got a job as a boatman and was employed ferrying workmen from the shore to mid-river where they were demolishing the old Newcastle Bridge.

Renforth's rowing career began in almost classical

Anglo-Canadian Boat Race on the Tyne.

fashion in that he was supported by that friend of the sport, the publican. This one was George Brown of the Battery Inn, Forth Street, on the banks of the Tyne on the Newcastle side of the river. Again like Clasper and Chambers who fought the cockneys tooth and nail, Renforth's great rival, who became his friend and played an important and final role in both his life and death, was a Londoner, Henry Kelley from Putney. Renforth beat Kelley on the Thames for the sculling championship of the World in 1868. Also like Clasper, Renforth's forte was leadership of a boat team; either a two man or a four man crew.

In the summer of 1870 Renforth left Newcastle with a four oar crew to row against the St John's crew in Canada for a stake of £1,000. Crowds assembled at Newcastle Central Station and cheered them off. The local applause augured well and must have carried across the ocean for Renforth and the crew won an easy victory and the Championship of the World on the broad waters of the St Lawrence River. On the crew's return to Newcastle the supporters were ecstatic. Renforth was hoisted on to the shoulders of the excited crowd and carried to a cab. The other members of the crew, Taylor, Winship, Martin and Adams avoided this fate, but all managed to meet up again at the Adelaide Hotel on Newgate Street to celebrate the victory on home turf – no doubt after their session the crew and their supporters were awash!

It is interesting to note just how highly the Newcastle people regarded the rowers. What manner of men were they? A verse from 'Renforth, The Champein' leaves little doubt:

'Tyneside's lang been fam'd for producin' greet men,
Luck at Airmstrang an' Stivvison, tee
An' Grainger that myed wor fine toon what it is,
An' its bildins thor grand ye'll agree;
But the bildin' o' boats an boat pullin's wor pride

An' where, always we try hard te shine –
An' Renforth, a brave hardy Son o' the North's
Browt the Champeinship back te the Tyne.'

Clearly the oarsmen were at the top of the tree, off the top shelf. All Renforth had to do was to go out and prove it, and in 1871 there was a championship across the ocean to defend. This time when the crew left Newcastle, a crowd of three thousand or more turned up at the Central Station to wish them good luck and God speed. The conquering heroes faced the New World with high expectations and great confidence in retaining the Aquatic Championship of the World. The crew consisted of Renforth's friend, the thirty nine year old Henry Kelley at number three in the boat, Robert Chambers (not to be confused with the famous sculler) aged thirty one at number two, and in the bow the thirty year old James Percy. As usual, Jimmy Renforth, the youngest member of the crew at twenty nine, was at stroke.

It was August, 1871, the river, the Kennebaccasis in New Brunswick, Canada, and the opposition, St John's, who were better known as the Paris crew. This was because the fishermen making up the boat had taken the Paris International Regatta of 1867 by storm. They had won all before them in their sea-going boat fitted with self-steering gear. Renforth's boat was the *Queen Victoria* constructed by the celebrated Dunston boat builder – not Harry Clasper this time – but Robert Jewett.

The scene was set for an exciting race between two crews on top of their form. Renforth won the toss and took the inside berth, and the race began extremely well. At the third stroke, Renforth's crew showed three feet ahead and after two hundred yards were half a length in front. All was going to plan. But a few strokes later experienced spectators could spot that something was wrong with Renforth. He appeared to falter and pulled out of his stroke – the rest of the crew maintained their rhythm and for the next few hundred yards managed to keep their lead. But by now Renforth was swaying from side to side. Clearly this was no temporary aberration. The Paris crew drew level and shortly after took the lead. By the half mile mark they had forged ahead and were half a length up.

Kelley, bewildered by his friend's behaviour, urged Renforth on. The Gateshead man tried gallantly, but the effort was too much for him and he sank back into Kelley's arms gasping, "Henry, I've had something". A contemporary report recounted the scene, 'The oar dropped from his stricken hand, his brawny arm fell like a withered branch in a storm'.

At once the crew abandoned the race and rowed ashore for help. Although Renforth was carried to the crew's training headquarters where medical assistance was available it was too late. Surrounded by oarsmen and friends, he died hours later. Due to his utterance in the boat rumours spread that he had been poisoned. Rowing had come to a pretty pass and supporters now expected foul play. The opposition would stop at nothing to win a race – and of course, in this case, the feeling ran, it was a simple matter of smearing Renforth's oar with something unpalatable. That's what had happened here, they thought, only the conspirators had gone too far and Renforth had been killed, murdered. In the aftermath of his sudden and shocking death these rumours quickly took hold. It was as though people could not bring themselves to believe that Renforth had gone, and so they clung to some outrageous theory as if in some way were it to be proven then their hero could be saved and everything would be back to normal again. Jimmy Renforth's crew would win the race and be champions once more. But Renforth could not be saved, he was dead and not, as the rumour-mongering had it, by poison. The cause of death was congestion of the lungs.

CREW OF 1871.
Top right, Kelley.
Bottom right, Renforth.

The body was shipped home to England and Renforth was interred at Gateshead Cemetery on September 10th, 1871, in front of crowds that were said to even outnumber the turn out for Harry Clasper's funeral. Again, the effect of a sudden and faraway death of a man everyone assumed was fit was all the more devastating. The mourners massed together in the cemetery for communal comfort and reassurance.

Far from being the fighting fit professional oarsman, Renforth was in fact an epileptic. As with Chambers before him, he was hardly in good condition for the strenuous sport. A memorial sculpture depicting the dramatic moment when Renforth collapsed in Kelley's arms was erected at his graveside. In the 1980s this was vandalised, an indication perhaps of how obscure the names of the Victorian oarsmen had become. Gateshead Council have since spent £4,000 restoring the memorial and removed it to a site outside the town's Shipley Art Gallery. The Canadians have made sure that he will never be forgotten by naming a small town in commemoration, Renforth.

There were other Tyneside oarsmen like Cooper, who has been mentioned for his battles against Chambers, Winship and Taylor to name three. But Clasper, Chambers, and Renforth were the men who distinguished themselves and the mere sound of their names acted as a clarion call to the river for the Victorian crowds. Should proof be needed, here are some verses from 'The Defeat O' The Cocknies!' written at the time of Chambers' death in August 1868.

'Aw'll sing ye a bit sang if ye'll join i' the korus,
Ye'll give us a gud un, – aw's sartin ye will,
For its all i' the praise i' the Coally Tyne heroes,
The Champeins we've had, an' the Champeins we've still;

Gravestone of Renforth dying in the arms of Kelley.

Tho aw's sad when aw think o' brave honest Bob Chambers,
Aw's glad the example he set's been weel tyen,
For wor bonny boat-pullers, the best ov a' scullers,
Thor lickt for thor equal – becas they heh nyen.
Noo it's mony a lang eer since game aud Harry Clasper
Astonish'd the Cocknies, an' myed them fight shy,
The Tyneside boat-rowers, se prood o' thor river,
Kept up the successes for eers its gyen by;
Then Chambers, the Champein ov a' the world's pullers,
Goh the Cocknies a gliff they'll nivor forget,
Whey, Kelley for six eers dor hardly gan near him,
Till he knew Bob wes deun – then he challinsed wor pet!'
But the Champeinship race is wor pride an' wor glory,
When brave Jimmy Renforth, se honest an' true,
Led the way before gud men like Sadler an' Percy,
An' the foaks that wes there sweer that he flew!

He's Champein ov England – then wish him success, lads,
May he, like poor Bob Chambers, stick weel te the nyem;
Then gud luck te the Fowers, the Pairs, an' t he Champein,
Besides a' the canny boat-pullers at hyem!'

EPILOGUE

The deaths of the three most famous Tyne oarsmen within several years of each other was a blow from which the sport never recovered. Professional rowing had lost its finest exponents and more than that it had lost its leaders. After Renforth, there was no one to fill the gap, as there had been when Clasper retired and Chambers took on the mantle. However, if there was not another great oarsmen in the wings, there was another sport for the crowds to enjoy, and it stole professional rowing's glory.

It was called association football.

In the last decades of the nineteenth century football clubs were organised, leagues established and the game which we recognise today came into being. Unlike rowing though, football was a game that could be played by children in the streets, the parks and the schools without recourse to backers, boats and money. It was cheaper and much easier to arrange and, of course, you didn't need a river.

The Tyne, busier than ever, was increasingly no longer practical for rowing. During the 1870s Lord Armstrong, in order to facilitate his ships' passage up the Tyne, dredged the river and removed the island of Kings Meadow, which had stood on the old race-course mid stream between Elswick and Dunston. Rowing competitively on the Tyne between the High Level Bridge and Scotswood was effectively over.

There was another reason for the decline of rowing, and association football, which took up the sporting mainstream, could well take note. At that time rowing was fast losing its clean limbed gloss. The cynicism of gamesmanship and cheating had invaded the sport to the point where it had become almost institutionalised. In the end the crowds could no longer trust in the fairness of the outcome of a race and had become disenchanted – perhaps the money at stake had finally fully corrupted professional rowing. The population turned to the fresher athleticism of association football.

Some of the reasons for the decline of rowing are uncannily reflected in football, our national sport today – fouling, cheating and the lack of sportsmanship. Falling spectator attendance is aided and abetted by television companies which buy up broadcasting rights to matches in the hope of promoting their channels. Like river racing was, football is a sport the nation professes to love. The lessons learned from the decline of Victorian professional rowing could apply to football – commercialism and cynicism can destroy a sport.

But the River Tyne is no longer polluted by industry and busy with shipping, there are people once again rowing and even racing their cockleshell hulls on the river and perhaps soon the crowds who once cheered home our gallant Victorian rowing heroes of the Tyne – Clasper, Chambers and Renforth – will return.